from Nancy Weber
Christmas 2021

A NEW LAND

30 Groundbreaking Poems by Youth Poets

2020

The Telling Room

THE TELLING ROOM

225 Commercial St., Suite 201

Portland, ME 04101

©2020 by The Telling Room

Cover and interior design
by Ashley Halsey & Andrew Griswold

Illustrations by Alicia Brillant

Printed in USA by Walch Printing

DEAR READER,

Please join me in stepping into a new land, penned by poems. This book, presented by The Telling Room, is a collection of youth poetry that is both brave and radiant. While the theme of the collection is emergence, these prodigious poets aren't just emerging from challenges and disasters—they are overcoming them, reshaping them with their pens. In a time where the threats posed by COVID-19, the climate crisis, and racial injustice might feel leviathan, these young authors still find the strength to imagine a new future.

The contents are split into three riveting sections. In "When We Began," the poets ponder family, ancestry, and the world they were born into. They come at the world swinging; in the stunning work "We Were Not Wolves," Kaitlyn Knight writes: "Being a wolf, pelt dancing. Being a girl, teeth clenched."

In the second section of the collection, "Where We Are Now," the writers turn their magnifying glasses inward, to interrogate themselves—their blood, their secrets, their multifaceted identities, and the wounds they face for walking in their bodies. As Mary McColley writes almost wistfully in "Arts & Crafts": "I love you. But / people aren't paper dolls, I'm sorry. / We remember where we're cut."

In the third and last section, "Who We Are Becoming," the talented authors hold fast to hope that is in no way naive. It includes their plans for what they will do once this "is all over," the bright light that comes from accepting one's sexual orientation, and the truths harbored by ghosts.

I find it ridiculous when poets are automatically waved aside as "aspiring" or "emerging" due to their age. If I ever doubted my conviction, this collection just further verifies it. These poems are vibrant and unforgettable, and it's a joy to read them all. It teaches us that in the white space between two lines, the pause between poems, perhaps we can break a fresh sheet of soil. Or, as the collection's Zainab Almatwari puts it, we can find "where two lands move apart / And the result is a new land."

Amanda Gorman
Inaugural United States Youth Poet Laureate

CONTENTS

WHEN WE BEGAN

WHERE WE ARE NOW

WHO WE ARE BECOMING

WHEN
WE
BEGAN

GRENDEL'S MOTHER TAKES THE MIC

Lulu Rasor

Listen up! I don't care for your petty battles, your
forgettable epics. Your tongues can't pronounce

my name, so don't even try. They say to name a thing
is to tame a thing, so I'm safe from domestication. Just hand

me that mic—while you still can. A tooth for a tooth, an eye
for an eye might not be your class of justice, but I make my own rule

beneath the murk and algae, over silver-darting slashes
and the endless sway of reeds. Where's your hero now, safely

sleeping in dreams of victory? Your swords and soldiers can't hold
me—I line my kitchen with the bones of kings. I won't pretend

I'm here for parley or peace. We don't have diplomacy
down in the mud and sludge. Teeth are the only treaty I know.

I'm unnamed, untamed, unnatural, unloved because I know
the silent death of womanhood. Mother sister wife

daughter lover princess queen—they stitch the world
together when your honor slashes it apart,

but who knows their names now? Tell me how it's worthwhile
to follow rules when all you get is a gouge in the family tree.

Names are overrated, legacies a scam—that's the harshest truth you only find alone at the bottom of a lake.

And here's a secret: wicked witches always have more fun.
I'm going down, but I'll claw my way into your epics anyway,
nameless as I am.

MATRYOSHKA

Lizzy Lemieux

I was born into a line of Russian nesting dolls,
each having cradled the next her womb,
curved from *shabbat* dinners,
a row of grandmothers in miniature.

Shoulders draped with shawls of a dying language,
mouths filled with chicken soup, paunchy stomachs
thrust forward after drinking two glasses of wine.
They never learned how to dance,

just swayed to cat gut violins and *niguns*,
studying genealogy like Talmud,
history's dog-eared pages clinging together,
imitating popery.

My stomach is skinny still, but I wonder
what to say to a daughter who will
separate rib from hip and mourn
words she cannot say, they've been buried
so long in graves with month-old children,
a daughter who treats synagogue like a cemetery.

I'll say to her, "Bubeleh,
Bubeleh, do not cry when you wonder
who sculpted that face of yours, your hips.
If you cannot believe in god, believe in grandmothers.
They all broke open for you."

INSIDE THE LIFE I KNEW

Clautel Buba

The Abubaca drinks from the Wubat River
and runs through my village, Balikumbat, in Cameroon.
Abubaca—
gray soil banks, monkeys hanging from fruit trees—
mangoes, oranges, papaya the size of my two hands.
The lines in my hands are like this river.
They bend and spread. They are the river and the long, dusty road
running along it from my village to Bamenda,
the bigger city.

When I go to the city,
I spend five days outside the life I know.
I see lights, TV, and running water.
But I am from the village,
living with my grandmother, next to this river
where the water is too dirty to drink.
We boil river water for cleaning and cooking.
Keep a tank full for drinking and washing.
I have big hands from working with this water making clay bricks,
farming corn, and growing up at age seven
from hard work.

I.
Dry season—
Christmas is coming, we are out of school.
It is a season for building houses.
Many friends work together for francs.
We work as such young children
from six in the morning to six at night.

We make the bricks by hand.

When we dig a hole so hard to dig, in cracked soil,
we use an axe. Blisters cover our palms until they are hard.
We go through layers of black, red, orange, white, and gray,
and then we start seeing water.
We cut through tree roots with a machete. Holes can be giant.

Water comes from the Abubaca.
Girls carry jugs of water on their heads, or, if they are strong,
they swing them to their shoulders or hold twenty liters in each hand
like men.
Boys pour the water into tubs bigger than we are
in a metal truck we push to the hole.
We pour the water into a huge barrel five of us could fit inside—
pour it through a faucet into the clay in the hole,
and mix it in the ground.
We pound the clay, frame it in wood,
put water on our palms, smooth it on the bricks,
pull the bricks out of the mold, spray dry dust on the bricks,
leave them to dry in the sun, cover them in grasses
so they will not crack. We lay the bricks in rows.

Someone counts them, won't pay for broken ones.
10,000 francs—not enough for a nice cell phone.
Christmas comes. We take showers, wear nice clothes, dance,
let off fireworks, stay up all night, waste a lot of our little money.
When it comes to having fun we act like little kids,
when it comes to work, we act like grown men.

When the sun comes up it's hot,
but at night we all gather around a big fire, burning cassava,

eating, and getting warm.
In the dry season, the danger is the wind.
Hunters build fires in the woods.
Wind blows and spreads fire to the bushes.
Dust storms bring twisters. If one comes in our door,
it can suck the roof off our house.
People get sick from breathing in the dust.

II.
Rain on the roof, wavy tin roof, beats over the corn.
It starts as a single note that you hold your breath on,
And when you take a new breath the song continues on.
When I was little I covered my ears with my hands and beat them
to hear the sounds change.
As you keep listening it sounds like music.
The water falls off the roof in straight lines
and dots the brick red ground.

The rainy season is a hard time, too.
It is the time to grow food—corn, grannut, okra, beans, cocoa,
cassava, plantains, potatoes.
At the beginning of the rainy season we plant corn
in big fields that we hoe by hand.
The land is huge and we are so small.
We plant corn as deep as our finger with our heel—
too deep and it won't grow, too shallow and the wind knocks it down.
Cover it up and the rain grows it.

There comes a time when
we take the grasses out that grow around our corn.
We break it off when it is still fresh and green and put it in bags.
We store the corn up under our roof when it is half-dry.

The heat from our grandmother's cooking dries them all the way.

Outside we play soccer in the rain, sliding in the mud,
dribbling through splashes.
My cousin and I sometimes take a big mixing bowl
from my grandmother's kitchen,
fill it with rain, and pour it down over our heads.
When lightning comes—it always comes fast—
and then thunder, we run inside.

Great puddles form in the road. Cars get stuck.
We push them out for money.
Sometimes people can't pay so they wait for the puddle to dry.
Danger in the rainy season is when the Abubaca floods.
It damages the houses we built.
Corn plants get ripped out of the soil,
beans wash up, cassava bends to the ground.

My life by the gray soil banks
of the Abubaca was inside the life I knew.
But we were like animals living in the zoo.
Animals who were born there.
The food they eat is the only food they know.
They don't know there's a whole forest out there
where they can eat as much as they want,
do whatever they want to do, go anyplace they want to go,
and be free.

UNTRANSLATABLE HONEYED BRUISES

Amanda Dettmann

My grandmother was known for kneading pasta dough.
Ribbons of watered-down flour elastically extended
from ceiling to hardwood countertops. Thin, edible braids
woven around her wrists.

She prayed in the dough, cupping her embroidered hands
into a quilt of promise where all days ended with open doors.
She counted in the dough, one two three, one two three
children lined up like feed sack dresses on the clothesline.

We were her boiling water, her cherished roots of ginger in oak bowls.
We were the ones gripping her fallen eyebrows,
her stretched out canvas-like skin.
We were the ones holding her splintered palms on crooked porches.

There were loaves of burnt sourdough on her back,
but she never wavered between the lines
of a baker's dozen and a speck of wheat.

Her faith a mosaic of plums coated in sugar, thumbs dripping
with trembling juice. Her patterned cheeks entire universes,
curled with constellations under the noses of revival, regeneration.

She finally swallowed our frayed scraps of sorries down her gutter,
almost blindfolded by our trails of squashed
dimples that never amounted to much.

My grandmother wasn't the kind
to be disarmed of lace

& we kissed her toes one last time.

BREATHING IN THE RAIN

Amira Al Sammrai

One time I lived
In a room with a window
I had to lean far out of
To see a small patch of sky.
I could hear the children playing outside
But through that window I saw
No sunlight and no stars.
I couldn't tell if it was day or night.
I was in a small bird's cage.

I remember one night
The clouds hugged each other
And the sky rained.
That night I hated to stay
In my room so I went out
To breathe the roses' perfume
And see rain falling on the paper bark
Of trees washed from the hot season.
Thin water flowed between my feet.

Back inside the rain fell on my window
Making a beautiful voice
And mixing its steam with my breath.
That day I flew with the raindrops
And I saw the gardens and deserts.
I saw farms, I saw houses.
The rain is a miracle of god.
After the rain eased

I could still smell it
And I went to bed
To sleep and to wash my heart again.

THE FATE OF THE TREES

Alias Nasrat

I.
An alley on the left
and a street in front
formed an angle
that embraced our home.

Across the street,
grass
and
sessile trees
stared through the windows.

I know
why they stared, for
my father told me once
that our house
was a field.

The empty land
brought us, the neighborhood children,
together.
We were home,
and safe,
as long as we were there.

We were the only ones
to worry about
the fate of the trees.

Otherwise, where would we hang
our swings? Or hide
from the sun on a hot summer's day
while we walked to school?

II.
I remember when we first moved
there was heavy snowfall.
Older children
took advantage of the land's shape
and built from it a slope.
I watched them from the window
or sometimes went along.

After winter, spring came:
The grass grew tall
and butterflies flew
from flower
to
flower.
The tall grass was
a better floor to fall on
than the dry hard floor of summer
or
the sloppy floor of winter.

When spring ended, summer came.
We hung our swings in the trees
or made ourselves soldiers,
firing at each other
with water-filled guns.
The older children did not care

what we did.
They flew kites instead.

Autumn made me feel alone,
not because my friends were gone—
there was something in the nature
of this season:
Maybe seeing
barren trees
and the sky clear...

III.
Now, years later
I live in another place.

Here,
there are three fields nearby our house:
One with full grass but no trees.
One with full grass surrounded by tall maples.
One with nothing
but tall trees.

When I was young, I wished I could
grow up fast.
Now that I am older
the snow stays a long time
and I don't have time
to play outside.

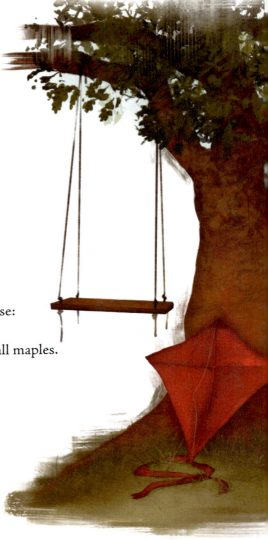

HUNTING FOR LIGHT

Henry Spritz

You knew them when they were bodies of water,
born from pine-tilled earth and northern summers,
raised on coastal rock and splintering piers.
As soon as they could find the surface they ran,
pulled from carpeted station wagons and the heat of day,
leaving morning and screen doors swinging behind them.
Pulled, spilling down wooden stairs, running over great lawns,
to crest above the blue, and the green, and the eggshell
and the rippling dark schools of guppies.
They could see it all in
those moments of weightlessness, when their feet left the dock
and the ocean seemed to sink back in anticipation.
From the stone to the sky to the sea
they felt the water rushing up their backs, into their hair,
pulling them into an embrace.

This is where you met them
when you were too young to remember, friends
with faces and names you have forgotten.
After seasons apart,
a decade,
the time it takes for a childhood to end,
you meet them here still.
Those who are swept up on these shores,
as you are, after so many tides.
Below the surface
their forms mix and become
lost with yours and the kids you once were.
Their bodies turn to churning water,

the pull of a current near your ear,
the presence of someone close by.
You paddle and turn among them,
wrinkled and sleek, eyes closed.
You are different creatures here.

Those kids, who went missing
summers back, for other states and other lives,
they could be swimming around you.
Those kids, dead or dying in the morning,
under a fluorescent bulb and different stars,
they dance in the thermals and murmur near you now.
Currents shift, bubbles climb, and you pull, pull, pull,
leaving them in the dark behind your eyes,
to emerge on the sunburnt dock.
Chalked by salt prints like ashes,
there they lay, the tired and the dried ones,
embalmed in light.
Faces wrapped in sleep and bleached towels
even then you can pretend they are the old friends,
hiding beneath worn skin and fresh cotton.
Even when the sun joins the game and is pulled under too
and the silhouettes trail toward frames on the hill, hunting for light,
you can imagine they are the old ones,
and you give their faces and names to those forms,
bodies you once knew in the sea.

WE WERE NOT WOLVES

Kaitlyn Knight

Placed among faces
with which I'm acquainted,
I find a time
when I was wild in a pack.

The sun rested and lent
the earth to its cooling brother.
That blind eye looked down on
five wolves, females,
before our prime.
The day was spent in celebration,
as was the night. Paws imprinted soft dirt.
Headlong we raced, young tongues lolling,
youthful eyes absorbing the moon-drowned road ahead.
Crouched behind bushes we lay in waiting.

We waited for the light-filled eyes of our prey,
speeding ever closer until our battle anthem rose behind us.
We charged, pelts glinting ethereal dances to the sky.
The car belted an energetic approval.
Startled by the noise, we fled, only to return to the hunt later.

We were not wolves.
Yet wild with our dim dances beside rural roads,
not to be remembered, nor found again.

Alone. Eyes glint only dimly,
darkened orbs that distract from keen teeth.

Precautioned people skirt left, right.
I crave only the life I live, with the moon and myself.
Being a wolf, pelt dancing. Being a girl, teeth clenched.

GEORGIA

Liam Swift

I remember packing my old school backpack
for our trip that day;
returning to the house to get the things I forgot.
I remember the early summer air, the morning
sky a high and whirring vacuum.
At the depot I watched you, a distant bob of yellow,
run to me from across the parking lot,
getting closer and closer until you slammed into me,
knocking the wind from my body.
I remember us clinging to each other
like vines.

I remember the sun-soaked hallway of the train station,
the way you talked fast and moved your hands.
Our faces pressed against the train window;
our eyes caught glimpses of fields from the seat.
I remember the train halting to a stop, you
pulling me from my seat and rushing to the doors so
we could be the first ones off; the sign,
"Welcome to Old Orchard Beach," was painted red,
just for us.
I remember taking the Amtrak magazine with me,
a pretty good steal,
if you ask me.

I remember going to one of the candy stores;
we could choose from so many.
Buying a squeeze tube of candy threw me off.

It was one of those tubes
that hold sunscreen or paint, filled
with a substance the texture of Elmer's glue,
the taste sweet and bleachy.
It painted your mouth blue, your teeth.
You asked me if your tongue was blue. It
was. Unearthly, chemically
beautifully blue.
It looked like the surface of the moon.

Most of all I remember your yellow dress.
I always remember
your yellow dress. How it floated
on the ocean's surface as you waded in;
a drop of honey in the blue abyss.
I joined you,
leaving the red-and-white Indian blanket
kicked with sand.
I forgot my swim shorts
so I swam in the shorts I was wearing.
I remember the wave
we didn't see coming; the one that
washed you up onto the shore.
You looked like a yellow tang
out of the fish bowl, delicate, breathing hard;
I don't know if you've seen one before.

I remember the train ride back;
How you fell asleep before I did,
waking up when the train reached home,
hugging you goodbye.
I remember you walking away in your wet dress,

the sky a mandarin blaze,
your feet bare on the pavement,
the dripping trail of ocean you left
in your wake.

THAW

Madeline Curtis

I wade through knee-deep snow toward sunset. Above me, black clouds boat across a flaming sky. The oak tree is bold and black, limbs stretch up as if in prayer.

As the sun disappears behind the hills, I think about a girl I knew a long time ago. We once shared a grape Popsicle under that oak tree, the sun buttery on our feet. Purple-toothed grins. Daisies twisted in her orange hair. Too shy to look at her face, I'd admired her ear instead. If I saw her now, would we be strangers?

Here is what I've learned: People change as quietly as snow melting.

WHERE WE ARE NOW

DROP OF MELANIN AND BLOOD

Benedita Zalabantu

I.

There's something about my brother that scares me.
He's black and a man.
He's a black man in a world where his skin symbolizes weapon.
He's a black man in a place where his skin symbolizes thug.
How can he move through the world
when his own skin is a shield for protection
and a weapon for destruction?

The way black men walk in this world portrays them.
The way black men walk in this world scares them.

A colored man walks with a weapon, meaning skin.
A colored woman walks with labels that will define her,
but can these labels be erased?

Black boy, don't speak unless you're spoken to.
Black boy, don't make a move.
Black boy, don't adjust while handcuffed.

At a young age, little black boys are taught how
they should and shouldn't act when they're stopped by the cops.

Black boy, breathe. I want you to breathe.
Black boy, you will be treated as a problem before
they realize you're human.
Black boy, keep your hands visible.
Black boy, be scared, but not too scared.
Black boy, you will matter.

Don't you know a black man is born
with a practice target that can never be removed?
Don't you know black bodies are weapons?

II.
My walk home with my little brother from
the bus stop is always interesting.
He talks about kindergarten as if it were heaven,
and I smile,
glad that I got a brother whose personality rivals my dad's.
Sometimes we see birds, sometimes we see rain,
sometimes we see snow. Ain't nothing but change.
But we don't often see cops.
One day we did, and he looked up at me smiling
as if it were his first time seeing a blue-and-white car before.
"It's a police car!" He jumped and pointed with excitement.
His round face looked at me, smiling with a missing tooth.
His little brown skin always makes me happy and I smiled.

He don't know yet.
He is going to be seen as a threat as he grows up.
It hits me: I'm afraid of how insecure
he will have to be around them,
around those who are trained to protect us but fail to.
I'm scared he won't be smiling at them anymore,
afraid he will have to raise his hands up saying
"Don't shoot,"
afraid he will have to say
"I can't breathe,"
afraid my brother will look up at the sky and ask,
"Why me?"
afraid he will have to say

"I'm unarmed, I swear."
I am scared because I know.
I know this is never going to end.
I know there will be a lot of reasons
he won't be able to breathe, and the cops
are one of them.
I know he's getting ready for a war that I can't prepare him for—
never really knowing when danger is around the corner,
never really knowing when dangerous is in the media.

III.
My melanin has meaning.
It is profound, dark skin
so greedy it gobbles up nouns, so tangled
look what it did to my hair,
reaching up to the sky at all angles.

To teach someone something about self-love
you got to start with yourself.
Your skin is not a dirty shirt that needs to be washed
like yesterday's shirt.
Your skin is like hot chocolate that warms winter nights.
Like rings around tree stumps, you have a history
attached to your melanin.
Never let the glaring whiteness blind you
from the beauty you are.
Dark as the night sky,
constellations are tucked neatly underneath your bones.
You know what?
When they call you dark as the night,
tell them without you the stars wouldn't have anything to shine for.
Perfection was not your destination,

dark girl, it was your starting point.
"Some say the blacker the berry the sweeter the juice,
I say the darker the flesh, the longer the roots."

DRESSED IN RED

Husna Quinn

The tapping of her scarlet
pin heels
fills the family room.
Her radiant red
dress illuminates
the faded gray shapes
of objects surrounding her.
My gaze
from just outside the door
follows her coal black eyes.

Glimpsing at the art
attached to the wall
she halts her steps,
ambling toward a conflicting frame.
Unlike the others,
neat rows of traditional prints—
drummers, dancers, and artists—
the family portrait
scarcely hangs onto the wall.
The left side of her faint red lip
tugs upward
as she observes the smiling faces
trapped in the photograph.

Her aura breathes "vile stepmother"
but her attire screams "fleeting lover."
As I watch from my post

in the black shadows,
my father saunters toward her
and embraces her pear-like body.
He pecks her red lips,
hugs her,
and rests his head on her neck.
It is a scene so natural and tender,
yet it has failed with my mother.

I close my eyes to them
and imagine my mother coming home
later that night.
With rehearsed countenance
she will imprison my father
in her arms.
She will hold him, and hold him,
long enough
for our validation of the embrace.
Detecting a lipstick blemish,
she will discreetly scold my father
advising him to be
more vigilant
in the children's presence.

I open my eyes and see
the color drained from the room,
the portrait still crooked
on the wall.

ARTS & CRAFTS

Mary McColley

I'm sorry. I never was good with glue,
let it coat my fingers like ghosts
before I ever fixed a torn thing.
There's too much of it between us now
opaque toxins clutching at our edges.
We're never quite whole, skinny lines
sticky as the space between atoms,
catching at dirt and acid dusts,
falling in love with bad things. It's not like that.
I love you. But
people aren't paper dolls, I'm sorry.
We remember where we're cut.

A LITTLE SECRET

Missouri Alice Williams

There was this girl I knew.
She wasn't very nice.
I met her in high school,
and all I can remember her doing
is slithering that cigarette out of her mouth
and going *pffffffff*
and blowing a little secret
to the boys.
She had blond curly hair
and then
the next day
she had black curly hair.
But
the thing I remembered the most
is that
whenever she would take her leather jacket off
all you would see
were these huge things
and all the boys would go,
"Yahoo."

PLASTIC PALACES

Siri Pierce

One summer
I met a seventeen-year-old angel.
She had a halo of burnt red hair
and wore a green and gold bikini.
She pressed a button and the garage door to heaven
creaked upwards and away.
Inside were bins of dolls and clothes,
plastic palaces,
and a big, shiny Suburban.
Everything I wanted
when I was eight.

Together we fought sandstorms,
became mermaids,
and drank peach iced tea.
One day, I made a ferocious tiger
out of orange marker and black velvet.
I bedazzled the bluest waves of the bluest water
on my mosaic.
Another day, I got a book and read it to the last page.
I never finished books
back then.
I was in the land of yeses.

I knew the angel for a week.
My mom called it "Babysitter Camp."
After that I almost forgot about her.
Third grade came.

Sparkly jump ropes, albatrosses, cursive,
and capitalism.
I still played with the dolls
she gave me,
but I had moved on.
I didn't hear about her again
until sixth grade.

The news came in a text.
A whole life gone,
captured in the ding of a cell phone.
Plastic palaces collapsed.
I had always known she was
an angel,
with her halo of burnt red hair.

SANTA ROSA

Abie Waisman

The outgoing orange of wildfire
Creeps toward Cedar Mountain,
A blood orange blaze
Slithering up the hill,
Snatching at a big, blue
House, chomping it away,
Then working down the slope.
A golden straw appears, drinks up the blaze,
And releases tide pool wonder water.

FLORIDA SUNSHINE

Raina Sparks

Tick tock. Load. Shoot.
Death was the hand that massaged his shoulders
built him up with cement and mortar and blood, fashioned his limbs,
      choked him
but allowed him to live, pushed under the ground in the Florida sunshine.
Three times. Four.

Her mother brushed the tangles out of her hair in long, thick strokes,
braided it and tied it with a yellow bow. Her white canvas shoes are now a
splotchy red lying out to dry in the Florida sunshine,
sunshine, created by thousands of candles in the night.

Rooms full of banned pages, because the only thing we can agree to
      ban in this country
      are pages.
The footsteps in the hallway sound like they are made by granite.

Education is not deciding whom to protect.

They spit back like hot pepper on the ones that stay,
on the ones that go.
Crickets.

We finally saw the faces of mothers with ash on their foreheads
and red paint on their lips
and in purple ghosts their eyes.

Seventeen, the number of breaths they took in the final heat wave
of Florida sunshine.

A DIFFERENT KIND OF BATTLE

Jonathan Rugema

There was always music all around
Gospel filled the morning air
Half asleep and half awake
Alluring and disturbing
Sent to bed at night, Gedeon slept
Behind the door I stayed up and listened
To the energy and laughing
"Stir It Up" kept me up

On Christmas Day, listening in church
A girl in the front of the choir
Erica's voice so soft and brave
It pulled me in, she pulled me in
Now on Saturdays, I sing with her
Years of Saturdays, I couldn't wait

Simple singing should grow
To more complicated singing
From background to lead
From easy to hard
But no, not always
"Teach me more"
"Just because your friends can sing
Doesn't mean that you can"

I can't sing?
Then why this passion
Why did you give me this?

"Brother, why do you cry?"
I cry for my passion.
"Listen to what I say:
Listen to what I play
The 'End of the Road'
Begins a new one
The Boyz will lead to Mars
Mars will give you Styles
I know your heart
Trust it"

Word gets around
From choir to chorus
Singing to playing
Guitar to piano
A different place
A different life
A new road
Smooth and straight

Smooth and straight?
Where do I go?
Signposts of shoulds flash endlessly
Family
Expectation
My mind
My body
The pressure of creation

Who do I trust?
Outside voices
Inside voices

What was hard, then easy, is hard again
A different kind of hardness
A different kind of battle

FOR WHO I AM

Salar Salim

"Terrorist."
This is what you call me without shame.
It hurts to be blamed for what I didn't do.
I'm here
because I want to live.
I'm not here to hurt you.

Sometimes I ask myself
Why am I discriminated against
for who I am?
I feel as though I am surrounded by ignorance,
anger, and malice.

You were taught to discriminate.
You say that there is liberty and justice for all.
Freedom is the state of being free, but within society,
why is hate your message of liberty?
Justice is fair behavior or treatment,
doesn't this apply to all women and men?

Battling to stay alive,
it was a struggle to get here.
At home we dreamed of America,
"the land of the free,"
but does everyone here
live an amazing life and enjoy equality?
I feel now as though it is all a lie,
the televised version, a trick of the eye.
"He's a Muslim, probably one of those terrorists."

This is what Americans assume.
But the Muslim person is here because he loves you,
no matter your religion or race,
not to bomb you.

"She's an immigrant, she is here to steal our jobs."
This is what Americans believe.
The immigrant is here because she wants to live,
and protect her children and not let them suffer,
not to steal your bread and butter.

When will you begin to awaken,
open your eyes, and discover
we all have the same aspiration?

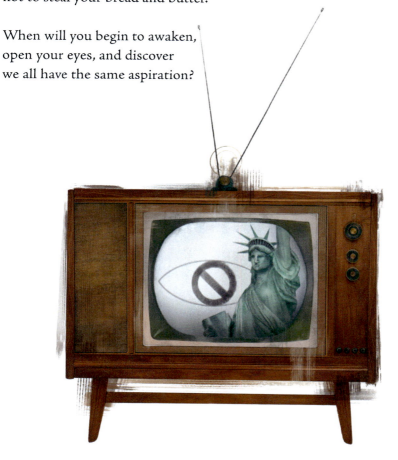

CRIMSON

Fiona Stawarz

Long blades of grass sway
As the wind roams.
Vibrant flowers begin to bloom
As the sun shows its face again.

The dark crimson bark of the tree
Protects the layers of tradition beneath.
It stands tall, though weathered by many defeats.

Birds chirp, unaware
That the blades that dance only by
Manipulation of the wind
Will soon be cut short.
And the dark crimson bark
Will be taken down by man to be used for things
Of the meaningless sort.

Just like the earth that used to be free
Of our feet, of our polluted ways, and concrete streets,
We are an endangered species.

In danger, we have remained.
Our thick manes and melanated skin
Are targets on our backs.
We have been laughed at,
Spat on, hunted, and abused
While the culture of our ancestors has been
Imitated as a muse.

Do we deserve no respect?
We've been stepped on,
Held down,
Knee to the neck.

A negro falls in the concrete jungle.
No one dares to stand witness.
Do his pleas make a sound?
Or will they be met with indifference?
Like the ground beneath us we have remained resilient.
It seems as though we are screaming in deaf ears
And our tears will never be seen.

400 years of bondage from slavery to incarceration.
We continue to bleed
And you continue to praise an America
That was built by our calloused hands
And on stolen Indian lands.

Unlike our tears
Your corruption will not go unseen much longer.

Dear America,
The eruption has already started.
The institutions that hold our freedom
Are begging to fall.
All those you have wronged
Now stand together.
Our roots are strong and deep.
We are tethered
By your cruelties.
Will you finally see?

Will you finally listen to our pleas?
Or will you turn a blind eye yet again?

This time we have nothing to lose.
Try and silence us.
Try to sew our lips shut.
We will still be heard.

Still we will rise
And your lies of life and liberty will become truth.
We will rebuild this country into what it was always meant to be,
A real democracy.
Mere fear cannot control us,
Our anger and sadness can lay dormant no more,
For
The power we have is undeniable
And change is inevitable.

WHO
WE ARE
BECOMING

YOUNG AMERICAN, ALSO ARAB

Sara Jawad

1.
born
into love and sacrifice
her father, her Baba, once said
she was "a child worth dying for"
he risked his life to get her milk
to feed her bones, to grow her heart
while bombs flew over their heads

her family pressed on in bravery
the crusade boomed outside
the door
her mother—warm, strong
a she-wolf—looked on
kept a peeled eye on
her daughters

her father
quiet in his selflessness
searched the rubble for hope
scoured the land to nourish the girls
he thought only of them
never of himself
"I will do whatever it takes"

the streets ran red in bloodshed
her father's crusade came to a jarring halt

he was captured
under the cover of twilight
he looked to the moon
"protect my girls" he begged
and his prayer leapt into the sky

2.
the girl is now two
old enough to believe in miracles
she took her twin sister by the hand
looked up at their mother
barely reaching her knees
grabbing her *abaya*
the cloth she wore to protect her from *shur*
and give her *noor* when she
picked tomatoes on a street once of trees
now filled with ashes and despair

out of the haunting stillness
her mother's phone rang
it was her husband's voice
her bag of tomatoes dropped and scattered
like marbles in the dirt

"where are you?"
she screamed silently
she clutched her *abaya* tight
her eyes widened and shined
like the light of a rising sun
her father's voice
almost unrecognizable
"plan a way to come to Syria"

he had escaped death
drawn courage from a place inside
his chest
his precious girls in his racing mind
adrenaline exploding from the
soles of both feet
he ran toward the border
risking it all
for the loves of his life

3.
fleeing
a thirty-six-hour trip
on a silent bus
filled with bodies
stories floating through the air
faces that had seen horrible things
strangers she somehow already knew
she could hear their eager hearts
beating

arriving, at last they could breathe
they exhaled
the greatest sigh of relief
her father appeared
at the border
holding their passports
between his palms in prayer
waiting
for them to arrive
uniting
embracing

shedding tears of joy
a family
resurrected from a brutal divide

4.
it was here
she lived her best life
six years
in an apartment that wasn't big enough
but with a brother
who was always there for her
she was never scared
her father
a mechanic and electrician
her mother
threaded and did hair
under the care of a safe roof
a home built from strength
filled with love

things started to change
Syria became her second bad place
the darkness crept in again
she was frightened
not for herself
but for her family that kept her sane

she heard gunshots roaring
like a hard rain
unsure if it was people
paying respect for those passed
or people being shot at

left for dead

"why" she thought
yesterday the whole country
was laughing and dancing
today the land is quiet
lives are being threatened
she worried for her life
for her family's life
she worried she might
never hear their voices
or her own
again

5.
at the age of nine
she fled yet again
only this time
it was right
but it was hard
she couldn't speak English
things were new every day
a heaviness was in her breath

but the girl was brave
braver than most
blossoming
she pushed her limits
she rode the waves
she lifted her head to the sky
"here I come"

from a newcomer to a refugee
to an immigrant to a shining citizen star
she was now every inch
an American
she earned her rights
she respected herself
she evolved
never looking back

today
the girl has a message
build yourself
create something
be painstakingly human
pray
become awakened
be unsatisfied
want more in life
let yourself shift
breathe
breathe again
be calm
be generous with the love
you give yourself

she lived twice
and you can too
a young American
also Arab

THE PRESUMPSCOT BAPTISM OF A JEWISH GIRL

—After Hanel Baveja

Lizzy Lemieux

We stood on the Mars-red railway pass
Toes curling over the edge, fifteen feet above
The river bottom stewing in August—
Rusting leather-seated wheelchairs,
Slatted red-handled, silver-wired shopping carts,
Old-fashioned, newly made, ten-speed racing bikes,
And children's tennis shoes with tongues like dogs.

The Presumpscot boiled like tomato soup,
Frothing with all these *things* we swam with,
Friendly with them as the fat, female ducks,
And their puddles of sopping bread.

We no longer bragged that we could swim,
But they knew—saw us wet and skinny,
Tan lines buckled around our hips.
We still screamed like children—
We still were children, I think, at twelve.

We hit the water with the sound
Of flesh on flesh, hand to skin.
We fought with the placid river—
Sometimes we won and we drew
The Presumpscot into our mouths,
Above Razor scooters and squelching mud.

In September it cooled and we sat
On the sloping banks with twenty-five cent gum
In our mouths, heads tilted toward the Vs
Of hollering Canada geese,
To which we hollered back
Call and repeat campfire songs.

We liked being heard, liked everything
Until our big sisters came home,
Each of their ankles wrenched, skin puckered, one
Hanging off a boy like a playground tire swing.
Then we listened to the water
Hitting flesh on flesh, hand to skin,
Listened to who we would be
When we resurfaced.

I'LL BE A CAT

Kaden Dowd

One day I'll be a cat.
I'll jump high and
I'll eat trout like a human.
But now I'm just a dog.
I have paws like a couch,
and I feel blue as ever.

CANTALOUPE

Emily Hollyday

Every day I wear my shiny red cowboy boots.
Sometimes I even wear them when I stand on my table.
I pretend I'm doing magic.
Sometimes I perform tintinnabulations.
The problem is my soles get real sticky.
No one cleans up their juice from their cantaloupe.

I always clean up my own cantaloupe.
In my house, there are lots of good bells for tintinnabulations.
Mom uses them to call us to the dinner table.
When she rings the bells I come running. My boots
help me run really fast, almost like magic.
Then I wash my hands because they're usually pretty sticky.

I don't mind being sticky.
It just means I've been playing hard in my boots.
I know how long I've been playing. Tintinnabulations
come from our church every hour. During Sunday school we feast on
cantaloupe,
and guess what? We don't even eat it at a table.
We sit in a circle on the ground and talk about God and magic.

I don't really believe in magic.
I just like to eat that cantaloupe
while I admire my shiny red boots.
I shine them every day so they won't be sticky.
You know how I told you about how I perform tintinnabulations?
Well, Mom yells at me when she finds boot prints on her table.

She says that food is the only thing that should be on the table.
Here's the problem: food makes it really sticky—especially cantaloupe.
When I stand on the table I pretend I'm God, using all my magic.
Too bad God doesn't have red shiny cowboy boots.
He'd look pretty neat up in heaven listening to tintinnabulations.

I bet you don't even know what that word even means—*tintinnabulations*.
I swear it's not some sort of wacky magic.
It means the ringing of bells. Like on summer nights when it's hot and sticky,
the bells don't ring and I don't know when to go to the table,
and so instead I eat my cantaloupe
at the playground standing tall in my red boots.

All you need are some boots and a little magic.
Sometimes things get sticky, and that's when it's time to go home, stand on your table,
listen to some tintinnabulations, and eat some cantaloupe.

ONCE

Madeline Curtis

My mother once said
She could hear the ghosts that shared our house.
At night, they'd kneel beside her and whisper.
They were children with faces like white stones
At the bottom of a dark river.
I might have seen them, too,
But I am not a mother.

A boy once told me
He'd swallowed the sun.
He revealed the warm red cavity of his chest,
And I saw it lodged between his ribs,
Fluttering like a trapped canary.
Do you regret it? I asked him.

I once caught the moon in a butterfly net
And brought it to my mother.
It felt like a rotting cantaloupe.
I looked and it was gone.

I once thought I heard a ghost whisper my name
In the cottony thick of dark,
But it was only the trees outside.
In their spiny, lurching shadows,
I saw how much I had left to know.

HOW TO BUILD A CLOSET

Jordan Rich

First, you construct the baseboards out of bias.
They build up around you from the moment you're born,
in all the little things people say more than the things they scream.
> "That haircut makes him look gay."
> "You're going to make your husband very happy someday."
> "Don't look at her like that; people will think you're a lipstick
lezzie."
The villains in all your favorite Disney movies are queer-coded
—Scar, Ursula, Jafar, all of them—
and the only time you see queerness on TV, it's a punch line or a tragedy.
You have your baseboards.

The doors are made of fear.
They sprout from the bias that has always
surrounded you and lock you inside.
Every time someone you love scoffs at the idea of queerness.
Every time you see old men on street corners or television
screaming, "Homosexuality is a sin!"
Every time a rumor starts that one of your classmates is gay
and you are *expected* to shun them, the doors get heavier.
You don't even get to know yourself before you start to fear what you
could be.

You fill the closet with shimmery, soft knock-offs of silk and velvet,
and these are the lies.
> "Yeah, he's cute, I guess."
> "We're just really good friends!"
> "I just haven't found a boy I like yet."

Whether you tell them to yourself or the people around you,
they seem to make the closet gentler, padding the walls and giving you comfort.
But the more you tell, the more the closet fills up
until they're pressing in on all sides, and you can't breathe,
and you realize they don't feel as good as you thought they did.
They're fake.

Acceptance is the handle.
You dropped it somewhere along the way in construction,
but you find it again eventually.
> Your mother smiles, says,
> "She sounds lovely."
> You can breathe again.
You use your courage to screw it back into the empty slot
in the doors of fear and swear the closet itself is fighting to keep you in.
That's silly, of course.
It's just a closet.

Finally, the handle fits,
the door swings open,
and you learn for the very first time that there is a whole world,
open and flooded with sunlight, right outside of the closet door.

THE TRANSFORM PLATE BETWEEN L.A. AND SACRAMENTO

Zainab Almatwari

1. The Transform Plate
Mrs. Fernald taught us in our Earth Science class
That there are three different kinds of plate tectonics
The transform plate, or the transform fault, is one of the three
That plate is between LA and Sacramento
Where two lands move apart
And the result is a new land
That is what happened to me

2. A Rock and a Hammer
The big rock that was in my way between Iraq and the U.S.
Was my grandma
The hardest thing was leaving her behind
She was the rock
But she was also the hammer
She said: "I trust you. You can do it. Just go."

3. A Small Fox
I used to be a small fox
I always had that sneaky part of me
That sneaks into the serious one
That part that told me to leave my goals
And do whatever I like to do
But after a while
I realized
Building a better life
Does not happen by doing whatever I like to do

But by everything I want to do
I can do it like a lion
Be brave
Independent
And go right for what I want

4. Maps
I expect from myself to draw the roads I want to walk on
All the cars, even the O2 that I breathe
I expect from myself to see, hear, touch, feel, and smell
I feel the reflection of myself as I can touch it
My new self gave me the pen to draw a street
That connects London, L.A., Tokyo, and New York
In my fox self
I thought those cities weren't mine
I thought each city was for its people only
My fox self was like a city in Antarctica
No name, no people, no feelings

5. Expectations
My parents pictured me as the recycling of their hopes
But with the goals of a mind independent and trusted
They saw me as the finder not the searcher of their lost moments
But I expect from myself more than people do
High dreams but I believe and I know
That I am going to reach the top
Even if I am short

6. The Transformation
I left the small fox in my backpack
She was the dictionary of my life
She was my Google Translate and my bad words

She was the hand that touched me through the continents

7. Altitude 39,000 Feet
I came with a heavy mind
Full of dreams
Goals and thoughts
Literally
I thought about the Latin numbers
The Greek government
The top of a triangle
The pictures of the tracks
The scary swarms of bees
I tried not to think about anything
While I was thinking about everything
Everything was pretty important for me

8. The Lion
I love my lion self
Even if I close my eyes and walk in the main street
Even if I say no while everyone says yes
Even if I tell my sister: "Don't talk to me for ten minutes!"
But I come back and give her my favorite highlighter
I love myself
I love me as a lion

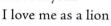

THE BUMP

Darcie Serfes

Life was simple before motherhood bumped into me.
I am unable to put back together the broken pieces of my dreams;
finish high school, go to college.

I am going to be a mother.
I am anxious, depressed, scared, trapped in a tunnel.
I hide behind a smiling face.
It's going to get worse before it gets better.
Be strong.
My baby can sense it.
Instinct is running through my body.

Cocoa butter doesn't work.
At seventeen, my body is not supposed to look like this;
stretch marks on my breasts, my thighs, my belly.
When I look at my body in the mirror it looks like a tiger attacked it.

I wish Madison came after I got my life straight;
was a college graduate, had a good paying job.
At the same time I don't think I would be in school
if I had not gotten pregnant.
I would be doing drugs.
Hanging out with the wrong people.

My mom went through all of this.
I would be lost without her.
She is thirty-five and already a grandma.
Both my grandma and mother are overwhelmed, but happy.

My grandmother prays and belly dances in the living room.
My mother tells me, "You opened your legs; now you have a baby.
I raised four kids. This is your responsibility."

I went into labor during the night and didn't want to wake anyone.
I took showers and swayed my hips through the contractions.
By morning I couldn't wait.
The ambulance came.
The men told me not to push but I couldn't help it.
We got to the hospital ten minutes before Madison Emilia.

I miss the feeling of being pregnant.
I love telling people about birth.
It's a pain only a mother can understand, and I survived it.
Room service at the hospital was great.
I had brownies with cherries, French fries, and pickles.

Now that Madison is out, I can't protect her.
I could when she was in my belly.
I am scared of Madison dying.
I had a dream my baby turned into a gremlin and attacked me.
What if something happens when I am not there?

My sister taught me to use my mouth to suck the snot out of my baby's
nose.
It works, but I can't do it.
My baby wails when you dress her, and she curls her lip when she poops.
I hate waking up in the middle of the night with Madison,
but I could not sleep without her near.

I am fucking up a little.
It's hard to focus on schoolwork.

I don't know what I will do now.
Maybe I will be a midwife.

I want to say it was a mistake
getting pregnant so young,
but it wasn't.

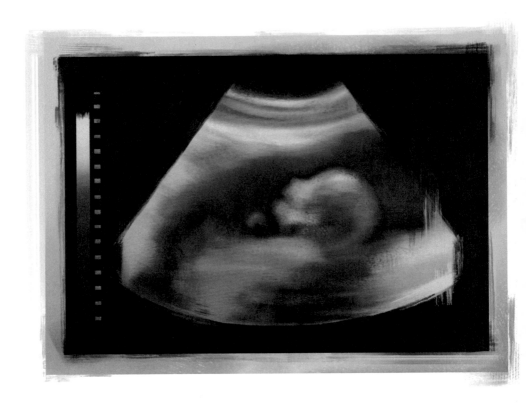

WHEN THEY ASK ME WHAT WILL BE THE FIRST THING I DO AFTER "THIS IS OVER"

Amanda Dettmann

I do not know what it feels like
to give birth to a child.

But right now there is a sound sizzling
every night at 7 pm
across New York
city
across rooftops
and gutters
and stickered bus benches

Clapping
for doctors, nurses, everyone
on the front lines
City as an entire
clap
City stopping to make the same motion at the same time:

A ten-year-old, clapping,
while her moon-landing puzzle pieces cartwheel
across the woven rug

A 45-year-old mother, clapping,
while her tomatillo soup sings
her engagement ring a ballet not of being found
but of finding someone who sees

A 98-year-old great-grandfather, clapping,
standing at his window with his bent cane
glasses so unfogged and unafraid it hurts a little
to open wider

How weird
for pieces of the body to choose themselves

for they have always known
foreign freckles
wrinkled, unrelated palms
cherried thumbs (not their own) sandpapering the same space they both
call home

Our dangling limbs touching each other
clap clap clap
so more people can touch
again.

***

There is a plant named bougainvillea.
I am naming my daughter
Bougainvillea—
the daughter we are all growing during this time—

because she will stretch taking nothing for granted into a new vine we call
Now
we call Monday afternoons at the office
we call nights sipping wine with strangers
Nothing will taste bitter again

Bougainvillea will thirst to say "Thank you," anytime, anywhere, with anyone
Bougainvillea will feed on firsts, a feast of anything, anyplace, any
moment, anybody

Because we have forgotten how starved we have been.

How a quarter of an inch of butter
did not mean a thing.
A paper movie ticket.
Scissors through hair.
Sleeping next to someone.
Sharing the same spoon.
Holding my grandmother has been a decade of drought
and all the water is yelling at me "Do it now! Do it now."

We are in battle. This
battle. To prove that Bougainvillea is a climbing plant
even when the dictionary says its flowers are "insignificant" and cannot move.
To prove that we are not machines
addicted to repetition addicted to repetition addicted to repetition

Our papery green thumbs were once
born as thin sheets of metal, once
gloved and greedy, masked and eyeless,
Our thumbs were shields
to touch
and be touched
to kiss
and be kissed
to breathe
and be breathed into

We have forgotten that a fly can still find its fire
even in capture and we are that fly.
Bougainvillea, you are blind now,
but I promise
you will photograph this world
in its most naked state of being:

black and white
no one is there
click, snap, flutter, flare

you will name a plastic grocery bag dancing in air alone on the street

as its own word. This.

ASTRIFEROUS

Alicia Brillant

"Fishnets," was all the scraggly, doddering woman said on Thursday night.
Her mouth twisted, slashed into a smile, the ridges of them
beginning to shrivel.
"Fishnets," she'd said again and again and again,
whispering until even the silence had become annoyed
to such a point, it began
casting her voice back to her, to fill its absence.
For she mustn't notice that it too had left.

"Fishnets," drawled the midnight sky, turning in and in and in,
rolling head over heels, for all the people below.

A few more fishnets for Friday, Saturday,
and Sunday too.
Fishnets, until the meaning of the word had left her mouth
and all that remained
was the implantation of the letters on the soaking ridge of her tongue,
in the far back of the cavern, at the very apex of her throat.

In the wake of her word, languages arose, like planets in the void, or
jutted landscapes on the Earth below.

Languages that the woman herself could not speak,
but somehow knew.
Like the bright blue plastic net within her hands,
which left behind slivers of parted skin and speckles of deep red ash.

"Fishnets," cawed the woman Tuesday night, shambling

down to the cusp of the waterline,
ankles shuttering and clasped by the wind that breached them,
hands curled far too tight,
around the light dipped mesh.

Taunting the damp sand with the horizon of her toes, she stood,
a smirk blossoming across the field of her face.

She raised her arms, up and up and up,
cast the net over the illuminated casket in the sky,
ignored the shrieks of stars and lamentations of wind
and all the protests that were suddenly below her.
When the other side returned
she clasped it, pulled and pulled and pulled
until the moon had crumbled from the sky
and fallen to the lake below.

She continued on, trailing for a few more steps into the water,
pulled once more, again and again and again
dragged that beast upon a shore
stared on as the dollop began
to swallow the grains of sand on the bed below it.

She turned her head from side to side
admiring her works done. The sky twirled on,
the stars scratched and scratched.
The moon remained upon the shore,
swallowing sand, drawing it into its heaving chest,
tendrils of light fleeing from its edges,
scorning the distant sky.

The woman went to the moon wrapped in fishnet.
The newfound child placed her hand upon its forehead,
smiled, and spoke:

"It's good to see you, old friend.
How about we speak again?"

CONTRIBUTORS' NOTES

AMIRA AL SAMMRAI is the author of "Breathing in the Rain," which she wrote at The Telling Room as a member of the Young Writers & Leaders group, a writing, publishing, and leadership program that brings together teens from many countries, including her native Iraq. "Breathing in the Rain'" was originally published in The Telling Room's book titled from a line in her poem, *A Patch of Sky*. The poem was next paired with Presidential Inaugural Poet Richard Blanco's verse in the groundbreaking book, *The Story I Want to Tell*. Amira is the mother of two young children and currently lives with her family in Las Vegas, Nevada.

In her own words: "Every time I read this poem it takes me back to when I used to live in a one-bedroom apartment gathered with all four of my siblings and my parents. I felt devastated waking up each morning; my eyes would shed tears seeing all the kids walking out to school while I couldn't. I felt left out of life as a child. That pain started to become motivating, and motivation turned into hope—for my siblings, my parents, and for our future. From that experience I've realized being grateful is important in life. After many years of enduring the trauma I've experienced in that period of time, it also got me to where I am today, living in the USA, a wife to my best friend, and a mother to two beautiful boys. The key to life is to turn your pain into hope and hope into motivation."

*

ZAINAB ALMATWARI is the author of "The Transformation Plate Between L.A. and Sacramento," a poem surrounding immigration of thought and body. It is a multi-award-winning poem on the state and national level, was originally published in The Telling Room's anthology *Sparks*, and Zainab uses it to deliver a journey that seems more common than ever to some and as foreign as an extinct language to others. If Zainab was anything, she'd be a "half-poet," as the poet Samuel Oguntoyinbo is known for in his miraculous poem "Epistolary." The other half is still pending, yet to be discovered.

In her own words: "I tend to use writing as a first asset in every situation possible, whether it's a heavily stupid pickup line or a detailed guide on language to refrain from using around a Muslim woman. Either way, my words and I are nothing far from conjoined synonyms. Watch out for my new book, sometime soon! Hopefully placed right next to Michelle Obama's *Becoming* and Tiffany Haddish's *The Last Black Unicorn*."

*

ALICIA BRILLANT is the author of the poem "Astriferous" and illustrator for *A New Land*. "Astriferous" won the 2014 Wild Words contest at The Telling Room and was published in *Maine* magazine and later won a Gold Key in Poetry in the 2015 Scholastic Art & Writing Awards. Alicia has since completed a BFA in Illustration at the Massachusetts College of Art and Design and is currently pursuing an MFA in Creative Writing at Stonecoast.

In their own words: "I wrote 'Astriferous' nearly six years ago. I have since grown as a writer and illustrator, but 'Astriferous' remains a relic of who I was, as a creator and as a person, and for that I remain incredibly fond of it. 'Astriferous' was also one of the first instances in which I thought critically about gender when writing. I can recall working on this poem and making the active choice to have a fisherwoman rather than a fisherman. This is a seemingly insignificant and simple choice, but it led to a consideration of gender—of representation and identity—now prevalent throughout all of my work. The other themes present in this poem, the variations of self and the passage of time, are also topics I continue to explore."

*

CLAUTEL BUBA is the author of "Inside the Life I Knew." The poem was previously published in The Telling Room's award-winning book of personal narratives about home by immigrant and refugee youth, *A Season for Building Houses*, which takes its title from a line in Clautel's poem. Clautel is also a musician and he writes his own lyrics, like the ones that create a drum beat in his poem: "Rain on the roof, wavy tin roof..." Clautel is a graduate from Portland High School who came from Cameroon, and was only here for six months when he began to craft his poem at The Telling Room.

In his own words: "It actually feels surprising to read this now, as it sounds so true about my village even after not going there for such a long time. It also got me thinking of my village, the life I lived there, and how I'll never forget all my memories there. I'm surprised, after reading the poem again, that I actually lived the life I'm reading about here. It really feels good after all."

*

MADELINE CURTIS is the author of "Thaw" and "Once." She is a recent graduate of Stanford University, where she majored in English with an emphasis in Creative Writing. As part of the Young Emerging Authors Fellowship, she published a book of short stories, *Yellow Apocalypse*. Stories from that collection won a Maine Literary Award for Youth Fiction and The Telling Room's Founders Prize. Her writing has since appeared in several publications, including *The Forge Literary Magazine*, and has been nominated for the PEN/Robert J. Dau Prize for Emerging Writers. Beginning this fall, she will be pursuing an MFA in Fiction at the University of Wisconsin-Madison.

In her own words: "With both of the poems in *A New Land*, I was thinking about the process of growing up. 'Once' is about the sense of mystery that permeates childhood, the knowledge that there is so much you don't yet understand, so much you have left to learn. With 'Thaw,' I was writing about memory and how life can change so gradually that you don't even notice it happening."

*

AMANDA DETTMANN is the author of "Untranslatable Honeyed Bruises" and "When They Ask Me What Will Be the First Thing I Do after This Is Over." The first poem was originally written during her Young Emerging Authors Fellowship and published in her 2016 poetry book called *Untranslatable Honeyed Bruises*. The second poem was written in quarantine during the COVID-19 pandemic. She will be attending New York University this fall, pursuing an MFA in Poetry.

In her own words: "Both poems weave together how we crave human connection, whether in a long-distance relationship with a grandmother or, especially, during a worldwide crisis. I believe this next generation is determined to transform vulnerability into our greatest superpower; unlike ever before, these youth voices are not afraid to write a revolution of risk-taking and resilience on and off the page."

KADEN DOWD is the author of "I'll Be a Cat," which was originally published in The Telling Room's book *Atomic Tangerine*. He is twelve years old and lives in Richmond, Maine, with his father. He goes to school at Richmond Middle-High School where he is currently going into seventh grade. Kaden enjoys watching UFC with his father. He got the idea for "I'll Be a Cat" by remembering how he loved to write, and then thinking about his cat Daisy, who was the mother of his cat Maggie, and his dog Stuwart. He remembered how Daisy would jump high up onto things and how Stuwart had very soft paws.

In his own words: "Every poem is like a child—first comes birth, then comes supporting it, and then it becomes whole."

*

EMILY HOLLYDAY is the author of the poem "Cantaloupe," which she wrote in high school while interning as a young farmer with the organization Cultivating Community. The poem was first published in The Telling Room's anthology *Call I Call You Cheesecake?* and reprinted in *The Story I Want to Tell*, where it was paired with a poem by Gibson Fay-LeBlanc, former Poet Laureate of Portland, Maine. In 2010, Emily received the The Telling Room's Founders Prize for this poem. "Cantaloupe" is a sestina inspired by Emily's childhood experiences of being raised Catholic and playing freely in her neighborhood.

In her own words: "For the past five years, I have been a sixth-grade science teacher in New York City. For my master's thesis, I wrote poems about subtle yet important moments that took place in my classroom."

SARA JAWAD is a senior now at South Portland High School and the author of the poem "Young American, Also Arab," a piece that she worked on in the National Arts and Humanities Youth Programs (NAHYP) award-winning Young Writers & Leaders program at The Telling Room. It was first published in The Telling Room's anthology *Speak Up*. She enjoys writing about her experiences as a new kid fitting into new countries, and this poem is about her life in Iraq, Syria, and the U.S. She believes in self-empowerment and never giving up.

In her own words: "Writing this poem and explaining my journey was like a weight being lifted from my chest. I finally got to share my voice with the world."

*

KAITLYN KNIGHT is the author of "We Were Not Wolves," originally published in The Telling Room's anthology *Beyond the Picket Fence*. At the time of that publication, Kaitlyn was in her senior year of high school and looking forward to a college career. She pursued a degree in English at the University of Maine at Farmington, where she graduated in 2019, before seeking a career working with young children who she adores and hopes will guide her in both life and writing.

In her own words: "'We Were Not Wolves' is a poem that never left my heart after high school. The friends that I wrote about are people who I love, and though we all have our own lives now, we love to get together and remember simpler times like this. I remember writing the last stanza of this poem with so much fear at the idea of leaving behind these friends and the thought that I would have to create new bonds. In the years since, I've come to find that bonds as strong as these may seem to fade, but, when it really matters, they always hold strong."

LIZZY LEMIEUX is the author of the poems "Matroyshka" and "The Presumpscot Baptism of a Jewish Girl," the latter of which is the titular poem in her 2015 poetry collection, written while she was in the Young Emerging Authors Fellowship. Currently, she is a senior at the University of Pennsylvania, studying English. Further poetry publications include *Best New Poets 2018* and *The Massachusetts Review*. Most recently, her short story, "X," won the Penn Review Fiction Prize.

In her own words: "Although I'm often inclined toward fictionalization, the success of these poems can be attributed to the old adage, write what you know. Together, they are a personal history of cultural identity and girlhood, themes which recur in my work even today."

*

MARY McCOLLEY is the author of "Arts & Crafts," originally published in The Telling Room's anthology *Sparks*. She is a writer and poet from Maine, currently studying history and languages in Paris, France. She hides in the corners of various museums and wanders the streets at odd hours with eyes wide open. Mary worked formerly at a lobster company and deeply loves the ocean, although she boils crustaceans ruthlessly. She draws and writes copiously, remains fascinated by languages and migrations, and speaks both French and English.

In her own words: "I wrote 'Arts & Crafts' in high school about someone who was, and is, very close to me. The bonds that hold people together can be very bitter, especially when they're mixed with love. I wrote this poem haltingly, with sharp syllables and line breaks. It felt like an apology as much as a plaint."

ALIAS NASRAT is the author of the poem "The Fate of the Trees," which he wrote in high school while working in the Young Writers & Leaders program at The Telling Room. "The Fate of the Trees" was originally published in The Telling Room's anthology *Exit 13* and reprinted in *The Story I Want to Tell,* where it was paired with a poem by Betsy Sholl, former Poet Laureate of Maine. Alias is currently working as an electrical engineer on the West Coast and traveling to different parts of the country for work.

In his own words: "'The Fate of the Trees' was inspired by my childhood experience and strong memories of my neighborhood in Afghanistan."

*

SIRI PIERCE is the author of the poem "Plastic Palaces," which was published in The Telling Room's anthology *Sparks* during her sophomore year of high school. Siri has been involved with The Telling Room for many years, most recently in the Ambassadors Program. She won the 2016 Telling Room Writing Contest and was a 2020 recipient of the Michael Macklin Fellowship for Poetry from the Maine Writers & Publishers Alliance. Siri is also the Youth Director of SolaRISE Portland and a freshman at Brown University.

In her own words: "I wrote 'Plastic Palaces' to reflect on a week I spent with my babysitter when I was in elementary school. My poem illustrates how my younger self grappled with death and the power and fleetingness of human encounters. Youth see and interpret the world differently. Poetry allows young writers to capture their distinct perspectives and share them with the world."

HUSNA QUINN is the author of the poem "Dressed in Red," which was originally published in The Telling Room's anthology *Atomic Tangerine*. The poem won the 2018 Telling Room Writing Contest and later inspired the Hawaiian composer Michael-Thomas Foumai to write an orchestral piece based on it. In 2019, the Portland Symphony Orchestra performed the piece alongside two other movements also inspired by two poems from The Telling Room's statewide writing contest. Husna currently attends the University of Pittsburgh.

In her own words: "My poem, concerning marital infidelity, is told from a child's viewpoint—a perspective not often portrayed in literature. The poem aims to raise awareness on infidelity's impact on children."

*

LULU RASOR is the author of "Grendel's Mother Takes the Mic," which was originally published in her book of poetry, *An Open Letter to Ophelia*, as part of the 2019 Young Emerging Authors Fellowship. Her poem was also published in The Telling Room's anthology *Speak Up* and went on to win the 2019 Maine Literary Award in Youth Poetry. She currently attends Oberlin College.

In her own words: "'Grendel's Mother Takes the Mic' was inspired by the Old English epic poem *Beowulf* and, more generally, my desire to give unnamed or voiceless female characters from mythology a moment in the spotlight. Because so many older myths are told in a poetic form, I feel like poetry is a particularly fitting way to explore those timeless stories through new perspectives."

JORDAN RICH is the author of the poem "How to Build a Closet." Previously published in The Telling Room's anthology *Speak Up*, the poem was written while she took part in The Telling Room's Queer Characters Camp. For this poem, Jordan received the Founders Prize in 2019. She is currently a sophomore at Bay Path University, studying Child Psychology in hopes of one day being a family therapist.

In her own words: "'How to Build a Closet' explores all the little ways external biases can get beneath an individual's skin—and the ways those biases can influence people's perception of themselves—through the metaphor of a closet being constructed."

*

JONATHAN RUGEMA is the author of "A Different Kind of Battle," originally published in The Telling Room's anthology *Speak Up*. He was born in Burundi and currently lives in Maine with his family. He graduated from high school in 2020. In 2019, he was featured on a Maine Public Radio show, "Music That Moves ME."

In his own words: "This poem was inspired by my love for music and the contradictory feelings of being responsible to my family and schoolwork and being indecisive about my future. I will go to college and hope to major in engineering, and I know that my passion for music will never fade."

*

SALAR SALIM is the author of the poem "For Who I Am," which he wrote for The Telling Room's anthology *Sparks*. He originally wrote this poem during his junior year of high school while participating in The Telling Room's Publishing Workshop. His poem was later published in the multicultural literary magazine *Skipping Stones*. Salar is currently a student at the College of the Holy Cross and is pursuing a degree in Computer Science and Business.

In his own words: "Islamophobia is an obstacle that my family has dealt with ever since moving to America. I wrote this poem to express my feelings toward the difficult realities that my people live through every day. I hope that through my writing I will be able to continue fighting ignorance and raising awareness of issues that often get ignored."

*

DARCIE SERFES is the author of "The Bump," which she wrote during and after her pregnancy and before she graduated from high school in 2010. She wrote the poem about being a teenage mom for the first time. It was first published in The Telling Room's anthology *Tearing Down the Playground* and then reprinted in *The Story I Want to Tell* opposite a prose poem by Lily King, award-winning author of *Euphoria*. Darcie hopes it will inspire other young women to know the precautions of teenage pregnancy and everything that comes along with it.

In her own words: "I am now a mother of four beautiful children. At twenty-eight years old, life has taught me so many lessons. I am a single mother, and I work full time. Juggling both has definitely been tough, but a beautiful journey! I still write every day. It's my get-away from my busy life!"

*

RAINA SPARKS is the author of "Florida Sunshine," which was originally published in her 2018 poetry collection with The Telling Room entitled *The First Rule of Dancing*. Raina will soon be a freshman at Yale University after taking a gap year to work on sustainable food projects. She cares deeply about poetry as a vehicle for relating personal elements of the human experience, and she is working on her second poetry collection written while living in the Philippines for the past year.

In her own words: "Maternal love is one of my favorite themes to explore due to its depth and strength. 'Florida Sunshine' was inspired by photos of the victims' mothers following the tragic Parkland shooting. My heart broke for them, and it broke even further as losses so deeply jarring to our national spirit failed to override corporate interest in policy formation. Our reaction to tragedy is one of those things that defines the soul of our nation. Gun control is imperative to any hopes we may have of finding our national integrity."

*

HENRY SPRITZ is the author of "Hunting for Light." Henry is a writer and filmmaker from Portland, Maine, who has written poetry, essays, a novel, and screenplays. His work has been published in several Telling Room anthologies, and his films have been shown in New York, Miami, and Portland. Henry is currently a sophomore at Bowdoin College, and has been working with The Telling Room since seventh grade when he published the novel *The Road to Terrencefield* through the Young Emerging Authors program.

In his own words: "I've been working with the concept of 'Hunting for Light' for several years. In the poem I try to capture that passage of time, from the way my relationship to Maine has changed to the ways in which faces have disappeared and resurfaced in my life. At its core, the poem is about how the essence of a place can grow and warp and eventually transcend the physical place itself, becoming a force that follows you throughout your life."

FIONA STAWARZ is the author of the poem "Crimson," which she wrote in the summer of 2020 as part of The Voice of a Pride series, which features works by Black and Brown writers of The Telling Room. She will be a senior in high school this year. Fiona has lived in Maine her whole life. She also writes fiction, to explore life beyond her world. Her short story "Illuminate" appeared in The Telling Room's anthology *See Beyond*.

In her own words: "After the death of George Floyd, I was overwhelmed and lost. I began working on this piece as a lackluster assignment for school, but writing it then became an outlet for me at the time. It looks at the connection between the destruction of nature by mankind and the abuses committed against POC in this country. It highlights not only the oppression, but the power and the ways in which POC are rising up."

*

LIAM SWIFT is the author of "Georgia," originally published in The Telling Room's anthology of colors, *Atomic Tangerine*. Liam began with The Telling Room in the Young Emerging Authors Fellowship and published his novel *The Sky at 5 A.M.* He graduated from high school in Portland in 2019 and has since spent time in Europe as well as working at a semiconductor factory. Liam will be living in Boston this fall, pursuing a degree in Film at Emerson College.

In his own words: "'Georgia' features a beautiful summer day that I spent with a friend, which gave me the prompt for writing this poem."

ABIE WAISMAN is the author of "Santa Rosa," a poem he wrote in the Writer's Block afterschool workshop program at The Telling Room. The poem was selected for a book of best writing using the theme color, *Atomic Tangerine*, in 2018. He is thirteen and going into eighth grade at Waynflete School. He has been a writer at The Telling Room for three years.

In his own words: "I decided to write 'Santa Rosa' when a devastating wildfire was happening in Santa Rosa, California, in October of 2017. The poem reflects the details of a wildfire destroying a house. But all of a sudden before the house is fully destroyed a straw appears and sucks up the wildfire and releases water."

*

MISSOURI ALICE WILLIAMS is the author of the poem "A Little Secret," which was originally published in The Telling Room's anthology *How to Climb Trees* and reprinted in *The Story I Want to Tell*, where it was paired with a story by *New York Times* bestselling author Melissa Coleman. She is still writing poetry and is also working as a teacher and fulfilling her dream of starting her own Masterclass Music Program for children.

In her own words: "I wrote this poem when I was a young teenager. I wanted to write about the older girls I saw in Maine, and I decided to focus on those who appeared to be bolder around boys."

*

BENEDITA ZALABANTU is the author of "Drop of Melanin and Blood," which was originally published in The Telling Room's anthology *Atomic Tangerine*. Benedita's poem won the Founders Prize in 2018, and in 2019 it received a national Gold Medal in Poetry in the Scholastic Art & Writing

Awards. "Drop of Melanin and Blood" is one of her many poems that speaks for itself.

In her own words: "'Drop of Melanin and Blood' is more than just a poem that talks about bias, identity, and police brutality. This poem is also about hope and fear. Through this poem, you can get a sense of who I am, maybe not a lot but it does more than enough. I am an older sister who fears for her little brother's life while dealing with her own insecurities. However, I pray that this world becomes a better place so he doesn't take part in a 'war I can't prepare him for.'"

ACKNOWLEDGMENTS

In thinking about a fitting celebration of the first fifteen years of The Telling Room, where we strive to empower youth through writing and share their voices with the world, we decided to focus on two things: The world needs more youth voices, and the world needs more poetry. Then, as this project moved from 2019 into a year that the world will never forget, we realized these young poets and poems had the power to create what we all need most of all: a whole new land.

Mining for a collection of "best" poems that we could bring together from thousands of poems, written by elementary through high school-aged students, inside hundreds of book covers we'd previously published, was a delicious and daunting task. We did not go it alone. Thank you to our incredible editorial consulting team, led by Telling Room publications director Molly McGrath and publications manager Clare LaVergne: Alicia Brillant, Madeline Curtis, Amanda Dettmann, Gibson Fay-LeBlanc, Elizabeth Flanagan, Megan Grumbling, Patricia Hagge, Mary McColley, Ladislas Nzeyimana, Siri Pierce, and Lulu Rasor. This team worked together in person and then in quarantine to do everything from selecting the poems to reading countless drafts of the manuscript to writing letters to potential supporters.

Speaking of such supporters, early and high praise came through such poet luminaries as Nyamuan Nguany Machar, Richard Blanco, Kifah Abdulla, Stuart Kestenbaum, Cate Marvin, and Gary Lawless, and youth poet readers Amanda Dettmann and Alicia Brillant. We are so grateful for that early confidence to keep at it. We also give our most heartfelt thanks to Steven Malk, Amanda Gorman's literary agent and to Wendolyne "Wendy"

Sabrozo, also at Writers House. And to you, Amanda Gorman, for being the person we knew would most understand the need for this collection and break soil with us to elevate these poets and their verses. Thank you.

Additional thanks to Alicia Brillant, whose poem "Astriferous" closes the collection, for their beautiful artwork, which accompanies each poem. The collection looks as great as it does because of the tremendous talent and aesthetics that drive book designers Ashley Halsey and Andrew Griswold. Poems were recorded by the authors in their own words in conjunction with the Academy of American Poets-funded project "Voices for the Future." Poet Laureate of Maine Stuart Kestenbaum leads the project and is developing a podcast with an ace production team—Sam, Josie, and Isaac. We thank you all profusely. Keith Cormier is producing an educator-friendly ebook featuring these audio recordings along with writing prompts written by youth poets Amanda Dettmann, Lulu Rasor, and Siri Pierce. Thank you, Keith.

While this text goes to print, a whole other team of people is working now and will yet jump aboard to help *A New Land* find vibrant audiences in schools, libraries, and shops, on buses and subways, and in your homes and ours. Thank you to Bobbie Bensur for dedicating nearly a year to developing the most robust marketing plan and materials we've ever seen at The Telling Room. We love that Shinebolt's Angela Smith and Jess Esch are pitching in to execute some of these ideas. And we are grateful to our book trailer director extraordinaire Steven Ciravolo and the smart, savvy, creative team at P3 in Portland, Maine.

Thanks always to the entire Telling Room staff, board, volunteers, teaching artists, writers, and authors who work so well together on the mission that brought us together and keeps us together, fifteen years later. We are led magnificently well by Celine Kuhn, through some of our most important and best years—thank you, Celine.

Our final and largest thanks are reserved for these poets: Amira Al Sammrai, Zainab Almatwari, Alicia Brillant, Clautel Buba, Madeline Curtis, Amanda Dettmann, Kaden Dowd, Emily Hollyday, Sara Jawad, Kaitlyn Knight, Lizzy Lemieux, Mary McColley, Alias Nasrat, Henry Spritz, Liam Swift, Husna Quinn, Siri Pierce, Lulu Rasor, Jordan Rich, Jonathan Rugema, Salar Salim, Darcie Serfes, Raina Sparks, Fiona Stawarz, Abie Waisman, Missouri Alice Williams, and Benedita Zalabantu. Thank you for joining The Telling Room when you did—some of you over a decade ago, some of you just this past year—to write and share your voices with us, for your trust that when we published your words that they would matter, and for your return to our doors, which hopefully will be open again someday soon, when you might run The Telling Room yourselves. Please keep writing, sharing, and inspiring new lands for us all. Now and always.

A Special Thank You...

Our writing and publishing programs—and this book—are all made possible by the thoughtful and generous support of many individual donors, private and public foundations, corporate partners, and government entities including, in part, by an award from the National Endowment for the Arts.

We thank you all.

For a complete list of Telling Room supporters, please visit: www.tellingroom.org/about-us/telling-room-annual-report/donor-list. Thank you.

ABOUT THE TELLING ROOM

At The Telling Room, we empower youth through writing and share their voices with the world.

We seek to build confidence and strengthen literacy and leadership skills in the youth we serve and provide real audiences for their writing. We believe the power of creative expression can change communities and propel youth toward future success as published authors, community leaders, and agents of positive change.

Our writing and publishing programs focus primarily on youth, ages 6 to 18. We welcome collaborations with other organizations as they make for exciting programs and events that would be impossible to produce alone.

The Telling Room
225 Commercial Street, Suite 201
Portland, ME 04101
www.tellingroom.org
207-774-6064

ALSO AVAILABLE FROM THE TELLING ROOM

A Season for Building Houses
An Open Letter to Ophelia
Atomic Tangerine
Because, Why Not Write?
Between Two Rivers
Beyond the Picket Fence
Boy In Bloom
Can I Call You Cheesecake?
Exit 13
Forced
Fufu and Fresh Strawberries
Hemingway's Ghost
How to Climb Trees
Illumination
I Carry It Everywhere
I Haven't Forgotten
I Remember Warm Rain
Little Bird's Flock
Once
Quantum Mechanics for Kids
Quick
See Beyond
Simona

Sleeping Through Thunder
Songs in the Parking Lot
Sparks
Speak Up
Tearing Down the Playground
Tell Me The Future
The First Rule of Dancing
The Presumpscot Baptism of a
Jewish Girl
The Road to Terrencefield
The Secrets They Left Behind
The Sky at 5 A.M.
The Story I Want to Tell
The Unraveling
The Weight of Objects
Truth Be Cold
Twelve Dead Princesses
Untranslatable Honeyed Bruises
We Gen Z Literary Magazine
When the Ocean
Meets the Sky
When the Sea Spoke
Yellow Apocalypse

www.tellingroombooks.com